D1797999

THE BUCKET LIST GUIDE ✓ TO FOOD

BY BLAKE A. HOENA

CAPSTONE PRESS
a capstone imprint

Published by Capstone Press, an imprint of Capstone
1710 Roe Crest Drive, North Mankato, Minnesota 56003
capstonepub.com

Library of Congress Cataloging-in-Publication Data is
available on the Library of Congress website.

ISBN: 9781669003694 (hardcover)
ISBN: 9781669003656 (ebook PDF)

Summary: Think food is the spice of life? Then check out
this essential bucket list of all things food, jam-packed with
ideas to take your foodie fantasies to the next level. Check
off each item for a full course of fun, like hosting a spicy
food challenge, starting a family cookbook, and more!

Editor: Donald Lemke; Designer: Kay Fraser;
Media Researchers: Jo Miller and Svetlana Zhurkin;
Production Specialist: Katy LaVigne

Image Credits
Getty Images: AegeanBlue, 23, Blend Images / Peathegee
Inc, 4, Caia Image, 13, Cleardesign1, 8, JGI / Jamie Grill,
17, Kingfisher Productions, 20, MoMo Productions,
7, Nikola Stojadinovic, 24, olesiabilkei, 9, Pamela Joe
McFarlane, cover (bottom right), Ronnie Kaufman, 22,
Satoshi-K, 5, supersizer, 6; Shutterstock: Alones, 11,
Andrey Valerevich Kiselev, cover (right), Arina P. Habich,
21, Artem Varnitsin, 18, Elena Veselova, cover (bottom
left), Foodio, 26, francesco de marco, 28, Ilike, 12, Irina 1
Nikolaenko, 10, JeniFoto, 16, kryzhov, 29, Maria Dryfhout,
25, Monkey Business Images, 14, 15, Teri Virbickis, 27,
wavebreakmedia, 19

CONTENTS

Words in **bold** appear in the glossary.

☑ LIVING THE FOOD LIFE

Everyone has places they wish to explore. Thrills they hope to experience. Food they want to **savor**. The best way to tackle these dreams? Create a bucket list!

Write down the things you really want to do.
Check them off your list as you enjoy each new
experience. If you're a **foodie,** this book includes
some must-dos to add to your food bucket list.

☑ IN THE KITCHEN

Every food experience starts with a recipe! Do your parents, grandparents, or friends make meals you can't get enough of? Collect their recipes into a cookbook. Then you'll always have ideas for something tasty to whip up.

GROW AN HERB GARDEN

Spices add zing to a recipe, but the real magic comes from fresh **herbs**. Grow your own basil, cilantro, and more! Clip off a few leaves whenever you want to add extra flavor to a dish.

MIX UP MOCKTAILS

As you're planning a meal, don't forget something to wash it all down.

Start with a **base** for your mocktails, like lemonade. Add fresh fruit (or even some mint from your herb garden) to jazz things up.

MINT MOCKTAIL

√ 2–3 mint leaves

√ 1 teaspoon sugar

√ crushed ice

√ 1 cup ginger ale

Place mint leaves and sugar into a tall glass. Stir together using a wooden spoon. Add crushed ice, and then pour ginger ale on top. Stir everything together and enjoy!

☑ WITH FRIENDS

THROW A PIZZA PARTY

Food is meant to be shared. On your foodie **journey,** look for ways to include your friends.

A pizza party will do the trick! Prepare the crust, sauce, and cheese. Then let your friends choose the toppings for their own pizzas.

DID YOU KNOW?

Halloween night is the most popular night for ordering pizza in the United States? Why not make some instead!

CAMPFIRE COOKING

If relaxing with friends is your thing, plan a cookout. Sit around a campfire while burgers and hot dogs are sizzling on the grill.

Once dinner is finished, roast marshmallows over the coals for dessert!

HAVE AN ICE-CREAM PARTY

Speaking of dessert . . . ice cream is always a fave! Like with the pizza party, you can provide the base: ice cream. Let your friend top things off with fruit, nuts, or sprinkles. Bonus points if you make your own ice cream!

DID YOU KNOW?

Ice cream is made from three basic ingredients: milk, cream, and sugar (plus whatever flavoring you might add).

☑ THINK LOCAL

You don't need to travel to try something different. Keep an eye out for food trucks!

Food trucks are known for their odd—yet tasty—mash-ups. One might have tacos with **kimchi**. Another, a burger served on **naan**.

19

VISIT A FARMERS MARKET

While eating local, don't forget about your neighborhood farmers market. You can find fresh veggies to top a pizza. Stock up on fruit to add to mocktails. Or get fresh herbs that you don't have in your garden.

FOODIE CHALLENGES

EAT LOCAL FOR A WEEK

Instead of hitting a chain restaurant when out for a bite to eat, focus on keeping things local. Seek out places in your neighborhood that you haven't tried. You might find a hidden gem while also supporting your **community**.

ENTER A COOKING CONTEST

Think your food is the bomb? Then see how it stacks up against other foodies.

If your cookies are worth bragging about, enter a bake-off. If you make a solid pot of chili, find a chili cook-off near your neighborhood.

SPICE THINGS UP

If you want to give your taste buds a challenge, spice things up! See which of your friends can make the spiciest—yet tastiest—salsa.

SCOVILLE SCALE

Scovilles are the measure of a pepper's hotness. For example, a jalapeño is around 5,000 scovilles while habaneros are more than 100,000.

You can make things even more challenging by asking everyone to buy their ingredients at the local farmers market.

WANT TO TRY MORE?

If you are looking for other things to add to your food bucket list, here are some more suggestions to try.

- ☑ Pick your own berries.

- ☑ Shuck an oyster.

- ☑ Brew kombucha.

- ☑ Make homemade tortillas.

☑ Grow a vegetable garden.

☑ Bake your own bread.

☑ Create a plate of stinky cheeses to try.

☑ Make your own salad dressing.

☑ Make beef jerky.

GLOSSARY

base (BAYSS)—used something as a starting point for something else

community (kuh-MYOO-nuh-tee)—a group of people who live in the same area or have something else in common

foodie (FOO-dee)—a person having a strong interest in the latest food fad

herb (URB)—a plant used in cooking or medicine

journey (JUR-nee)—a long trip or experience

kimchi (KIM-chee)—a spicy vegetable dish that has of one or more pickled vegetables, especially cabbage

naan (NAHN)—a round, flat bread popular in India

savor (SAY-vur)—to taste or smell with delight

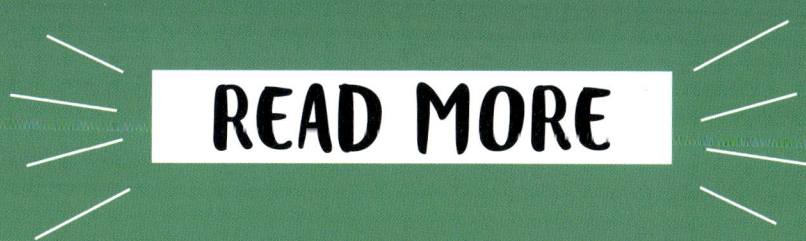

READ MORE

Catherman, Jonathan. *The Manual to Middle School: The "Do This, Not That" Survival Guide for Guys*. Grand Rapids, MI: Revell, 2017.

Crohn, Joann. *Me and My Friendships: A Kid's Guide to Making and Being Friends*. Emeryville, CA: Rockridge Press, 2021.

Newman, Catherine. *How to Be a Person: 65 Hugely Useful, Super-Important Skills to Learn before You're Grown Up*. North Adams, MA: Storey Publishing, LLC, 2020.

INTERNET SITES

100+ Things for Teens to Do This Summer
studentden.com/100-things-for-teens-to-do-this-summer

How to Handle Peer Pressure
kidshealth.org/en/kids/peer-pressure.html#catfriend

Young Men's Health: Friendship Issues
youngmenshealthsite.org/guides/friendship

INDEX

ABOUT THE AUTHOR

Blake A. Hoena grew up in central Wisconsin, where he wrote stories about robots conquering the moon and trolls lumbering around the woods behind his parents house. He now lives in Minnesota and enjoys writing about fun things like history, space aliens, and superheroes. Blake has written more than fifty chapter books and dozens of graphic novels for children.